I LOVE YOU IS BACK
DERRICK C. BROWN

Write Bloody Publishing ©2006

SPECIAL THANKS FOR HELPING THIS BOOK COME TOGETHER:

AMANDA VALENTINE

BUDDY WAKEFIELD

MATT MAUST

TAYLOR MALI

STEPHEN LATTY

JANET FITCH

BRANDON LYON

NATHAN WARKENTIN

Major Thanks to The Blacksmith Collective.

5th printing.

Printed in NASHVILLE TN USA

AUTHOR'S NOTE

I LOVE YOU IS BACK

*I was walking through a late New York City weeknight with acclaimed
poet Mike McGee. We had been dancing ridiculously with the brilliant poets of the
Bowery Poetry Club and The Louder Arts lushes from Bar 13. We were in the mood.
You know that mood,
when no one leaves early, no wallflowers are left, the dancing escalating
into prime morning conversation embarrassment.*

*Mike and I began officially wandering the streets. I love wandering… when I have
money to get home.
That night I had some.
I think we were near 14th st. and Blasted. We found some graffiti.
We stared at it until booze tears welled up a little.
He took a photo of it. It became the title of this book.
You should make someone's day by posting the phrase somewhere.*

*Here's to not getting caught, here's to writing like you're posessed,
here's to you being nuts,*

D.

Designed by Matt Maust
All Illustrations by Derrick C. Brown

One must pass through
life, red or blue, quite
naked, with the music
of the subtle sinner, at
all times ready to
party.

Only those who contemplate
the constellations
can still move us.

-Francis Picabia

To all the ones wondering if they are actually writers,
the wondering says you already are.
The details you noticed says you always were.
Rewriting, questioning and kicking in doors means
you'll be good.

-D

I LOVE YOU IS BACK

I LOVE YOU IS BACK

ALL DISTORTION, ALL THE TIME

Someone plug my lungs back into the guitar amps!
I want to live on
All distortion, all the time.

Aren't you sick of being appraised as just wholesale?
Aren't you sick of sailing on listing ships?
Aren't you weary from playing cellos with ex-lover's bones?

I want the butterfly brigade to grant me a year with no stomach drama.
I want a piano that will not warp outdoors
when the rain demands slow dancing.

I want to skew the difference between Tai Chi and Chai tea,
and end up drinking a tall glass of your graceful force.
I want to lick my hands after I touch someone that has just become
razzle dazzled by tomorrows oncoming lightning.
I want birds to come close enough to hear them speak Aviation Spanish.

"Abierto! Abierto!"

I want your record collection in my throat,
and my thumb in the electric ass of the all night jukebox.

I want my shoulder blades mounted in the museum of the most fantastic knives.

I want church in a bar. I want to pass out and hear you say Amen.
I want a skeleton night light in the closet.
I want your wow in my now so we become NWOW.
I want the light in your attic to shine down to where the sidewalk ends.
I want free shit to not cost anything. That'd be nice.
I want you to feel like a disco ball of fish hooks
so you can hang on my words and I can spin in your small miracles of light.

I want my kitchen to be a Brazilian dance floor
with a pot of your sweat in the oven
and a fridge stocked with booty lust.

I want your silver muscles cut into a quilt. Let me sleep under your strength.
I want more pony lamps. No reason.

I want to sing this feeling into all tail pipes
until I'm exhausted.

I want to smell everything.
I want to remember that the sky is so gorgeously large,
I feel stranded beneath it.

When I gasp beneath it,
I only want to gasp for more.

SAINT MARK'S

The telephone wires must be down.

You still haven't called this winter.

I decide to go to the church,
the empty one
that looks like it was struck by meteors.

I see it from Highway 31, off the road a little bit. Spring Hill.

The roof has blown off of the Tennessee Assembly of God,
formerly known as Saint Marks.

I go in with a camera.
I hope to replace some dated photographs in my home.

The backdoor is unlocked and the carpets are flooded.
Grass is clawing through the floorboards.
Red plastic flowers on their side.

There is a sycamore in the parking lot
whose leaves will not let go.

Fake stained glass decals and pews broken by axes.
Hymnals warped.

There is a dove design
on the hymnal. I once saw it on a shotgun barrel.
There is a song in here calling for that lightning bolt,
the one that is still trying to land on my fork.
There is a field, with no one to run to on the other side
and no reason to return to the start. Above me, through the rafters, a flock
    of vultures.
Death is humming hymns from the air conditioner
and the mantis' in the walls pray for my soul.

This church was great.

I return home to a room without.
My bedroom is a supermarket that is running out of food.
Aisles of non-unique orgasms and flailing spirits.
None of them want to check out.
All of them smelling shampoo bottles without realizing it's all got the same stuff inside.

There's a plastic orange skyline of pill bottles on the nightstand.
There's a photograph of someone forcing a smile.
The sheets only warm my nightmares.
I still sleep on my side of the bed
in case she ever comes back.

A chapel fills with snow.

Hallelujah.

THE UNCAPTURED ORCHESTRA

The chubby girl is struggling speed on roller skates.

She is alone.
She is in that crazed eye.
She imagines the neighborhood friends.

Most the poets I know are fat girls on roller skates.
They have all the gear and don't actually use it.

Few of them are in love,
but many know how to stumble and sing
the notes of the uncaptured orchestra.

I think the composer Randy Newman is like that.
I don't think he loves L.A.
I don't think he loves.
I don't think I really have a friend in him.

The friends I know
who are in love
are doing something.

Love is busy magic.

Love must be magic
'cause when my friends fall in it
they disappear.

I drove with a woman
across the mosquito creeks of Arkansas
to figure out why that was.

Looking at each other like surgeons,
daring the other to go first,
I finally asked how long
she thought it would last.

She said she it didn't matter how long,
it just mattered that it was.

I changed the subject,
told her about the lone roller skater.
I asked if she thought she had ever been kissed.
She didn't think so.

We held still, then

a sky flush with moon
opened up like a ballroom
and her kiss broke the spine of the night,
paralyzing the moment
into our skulls,
forever.

SHOWER POWER

Do not be ashamed
that you must take marathon showers
in your morning.

Sing out full blast in that steamy confessional.
Crank up that husky turbine.

As water sprays the plastic shower curtain,
hear it as the distant applause
of an astounded Carnegie Hall audience.
If your neighbors are not astounded,
then you got dirty neighbors.

I myself need twenty minutes of applause to feel
like the day
is a deserving encore.

And the spiders that snuck in through the drain
will die spinning, soaked dervishes,
flighting to stick one last web to pull further from dark death
and closer to the splendor and gleam
of your fading melody.

Pour out a splash of shampoo for dead bugs everywhere.

The least we can do for them is a song.

SHE BLEEDS INTO SURF

When I go to the beach I see: dogs spinning salt water from their fuzz and tan chess pieces turtling on cruisers. I see the poor in their underwear swatting at the whitewash. Bikinis blast their sexed and silent colors up from the monotone stoves of sand.
During this time, I was moved when I saw a woman bleed while surfing.

She took a surfboard scag in the rib.
I saw the red exiting a route from her flesh
and watched it mix with the water like milk and tea.

I know she wondered about the beasts below, with horror ignited,
streaming teeth towards her soft-soft-
but she kept going.

Sometimes the sea is a surprise.
I watched it power her face down into sandbars,
air escaping her chest in an undersea arm wrestle,
soon racing to the victory of sunlight.

What woman doesn't dance and power through her own damage recital?
What woman doesn't sneer blood and feel the sea as something inside
when she notices the point where all water goes dark?

She twisted hotly with a barbershop razors grace.
The body's smooth command over slobbering mouths of blue,
cutting through hysterical green.

Women are of the sea. A sea hypnotized by the moon.
A daughter of Jack the Ripper found her home slicing the water's skin with
surfboards, balancing solo across beams of horizon
where sea hollows out and becomes sky.

Standing in a feeling as alone as an old folks home.
Harnessing action from those curling chariots,
shaking something unspoken from her spirit.
Something no doctor could touch.

This ancient liquid crushes, bludgeons itself into white
and spits splinters of millions of ships,
ships that gave in to it's darkness.

Skeletons of sailors lay on their spines to watch her shadow pass overhead.
Yes. Yes. Come.

This sea chooses not when it will soothe or destroy it's guests.
It only does.

This too, is her.
Straddling the board a half-mile out, she cups a few ounces of sea in her hand;
wonders how old that portion of water is
and lets it sift through her fingers.

The sea is not where we trespass,
but rather, a drama where we belong.

A sea that once was merciless to subs and lurched over armadas,
seems to understand the power of two forces
and soon bows down
with a woman
on top
of its throat

MY FIRST CPR CLASS

We met at a CPR class for singles.

We learned that the inhalation phase of breathing
is called inspiration.

She said, "If you breathe into someone else,
it should be called something more magical."
I said, "Like expiration?"
She said, "Something more spiritual."
I said, "Resperado."

We met at a CPR class for singles.

We both showed up early for the poison healing chapter.

During drills, I volunteered to choke.
She volunteered to Heimlich me.
Her tense arms reached around me like a semi-heterosexual cowboy
and pulled hard.
I coughed out a Tic-Tac from the day before and told her it was a tooth.
She said, "Your teeth smell minty."
I said, "That's the nicest thing a non-dentist has ever said to me."

We met at a CPR class for singles.

She was all dressed up in blue emergency.
Styled in the symptoms of shock.
I wanted to tell her some poetic madness,
a vagina wrangling phrase like:
"You are a swinging peppermint nightstick of pink,
crashed on all my horny bionics."

All that came out was,
"Hey, isn't it funny how old people really love pie?"

She said, "Isn't it beautiful how old people respect every breath.
We breathe 17 times per minute."
I said, "Less if sleeping."
She said, "Less if kissing."
I said, "And um, or... snorkeling?"

We practiced mouth to mouth on the dummy.
She said she was used to making out with the brainless.
She dropped her gum in its mouth as a joke... for me to find.
I had a hard time retrieving it with my tongue.
I got it after five minutes.

The instructor suspended me from further oral interactions
with all plastic devices within the room.

When it came time for a live volunteer to mimic an unconscious stroke victim,
I beat her to it. I laid down.
She stepped up and I closed my eyes.
I liked her mouth, docking upon mine in its Armenian grip.
I felt upon my lips, her 'I might look like a cop in 24 years" mustache and
knew we had something in common, and that something was justice.

I moved her down to mine.
We kissed like Europeans who just discovered that it's O.K. to put ice in a coke,
The gum fell into my throat and I actually choked.
The instructor thought I was getting into the drill again and kept the class coming.
A dude with a beard made of tuna fish, breathed into me like a diesel leaf blower.
A nineteen-year-old girl with a goiter and no upper lip breathe-sneezed into me
wetter than an whale porno.
Then a short, spandexed man who looked like Boris Yeltsin's dead baby
slobbered into my tonsils until he pressed his gold ringed hands on my chest
and the Big League Chew rocketed out like a geyser.

We met at a CPR class for singles.

I learned that a mouth finding another mouth
in it's desperate gaping,
could land and surrender to shared air,
and the thing that passes between mouths as the lips connect
could save your life.

...that and massive pumping on the breasts .

THE PARTY

It's just a room full of expensive postcards.
These people are brilliant
like perfumed fish scales.

The aerial maneuvers of the elite
hold no grace for me.

I understand the ballet of dragging your ass through the mud
much more than this dance of constant glistening.

Let's go drink whiskey in the park at lunch.
Let's eat everything in your cupboard before shopping again.
Let's ask for a good citizen's discount.
Let's sneak into a hotel pool and do the dead man's float.
Let's sell some clothes and cd's for wine money.

The poor don't go extinct.

RECORDING TEXT BOOKS FOR THE BLIND

I had never gone inside the blind mans house before.
I had read his graduate text books on Astronomy, Polynesian music theory
and strange mathematics into a tape recorder.
All mumbled for him for five bucks an hour in Flagstaff.
I thought it would be nice to work from home and help someone.

It dragged on me.

After two hours of recording
I would begin skipping things that seemed unimportant... to me.

I also added jokes about various pictures in the book.
"And this is a picture of a naked lady. What's that doing in here, and what is
    she doing to that coconut?"
I never told him that I skipped some stuff.

He couriered a message to me to bring a 40 watt light bulb
and that I would be reimbursed
during my next tape delivery.
When I arrived he asked me to help him replace it
so he wouldn't get shocked.
After a few seconds,
I wondered why I was replacing a light bulb in his house.
He said he could tell a difference.

The place seemed cozy to me.
I asked him if it felt like home.
He said nowhere felt like home.

I asked him the most pedestrian of questions, "What's it like?"

"Oh, living alone?"

It's not what I meant but I listened.
He said when you are alone you drink slower.
He said he had a bottle made of bone and how different it felt on his lips
    compared to ceramic.
He says when he speaks now, more often he means what he says.

Of course I wanted to know about living with blindness.
I wanted to tell him I wrote a story about a time when I was an Easter bunny
    for some blind kids,
as if that would make us feel bonded.

He mentioned that all he has ever learned about stars rolling in gas,
The sound of Hawaii and various algorhythms come to his brain as my voice.
He said I was in his head and that when I spoke, he expected a load of random
    information.
I kept moving my hand near him, gently.
I kept trying to tell if he could tell that I was looking at him.

Standing there at his door I tried to tell him
how cold I was because I wasn't wearing a jacket.
 I must've sounded nervous.
 His record player was dusty.
I didn't know if I should tell him.

I asked him one night,
dropping off the cassette, what he dreamt about.
 He said each word crisply:

"Shapes.
Mostly shapes.
And a woman.

How are the light bulbs doing?"

WOLVES A- TWITCH A- GO- GO

I will meet you at the Yum Yum Dance Hall.

I parked so far I forgot my name.

I closed my eyes
joined in on the dance floor full
of people with clear chests.

Undersexed people had rope lights lining their ribcages
and you could see a piece of raw meat
hanging in there like a sleeping bat.

So many chest lights.
All were dancing as fast and as manic as they could.
To heat their bodies up
so they could cook that dangling meat
and serve it back to the cow who was DJ'ing
songs about where all the meadows went.

A gypsy in the corner was rolling around
in a ball pit full of sleeping pills.
She said, "Never trust a monkey to do your laundry.
You just walk around looking dirty to everyone.
Look, I hooked up the wolf over there with a little snoozefest."

There was a wolf in a cage
sleeping with his legs a-twitch.
They must be nightmares set by the pills.
Meadow songs soothed over him with bass.

All the dancers moved around his fur
ignoring the possibility of waking
the black gums and frozen snarl.

I wonder if the wolf dreams of a world with no doorbells or trumpets.
A skyscraper made of sweet dog shit.
Cats and squirrels without legs.

A wall made of fingers to rub and lurch against.
Being hungry in the snow.
Being in front of a classroom with no fangs on.
Someone dressing you in a bandanna and small pants with a tail hole.
Purple bedazzled muzzles.
Everyone talking to it like it was a child.

Asleep, its body goes:
A-twitch twitch twitch.

In the restroom I realized
I finally made the cover of the outhouse catalogue.
An article about how I've treated people.
An ad about where the real ME went.

Fine.
Every night that I feel like I'm losing touch
with who I really am,
I realize I really am the kind of guy
who loses touch with who he is.

On the dance floor,
Black cops grinded white motorcycles.
The Mayor of Yum City was in the VIP booth mentioning
that the squid invasion had begun.
Calamari is back!
Meadow music is back!

I say, I love you is back.
There is a pause.
His whole booth gets up and says
"I love you is front. Don't front from the back."

As they exit the MC makes an announcement:
"All ammo junkies report to the super model firing squad.
Someone soft will french your revolver and...
 to the owner of a blue Honda Accord, you left your nipples on."

The one I want is out there, cooking her meat.
She will pump oxygen into my Vegas showroom.
I don't know if possibly, I'm in love,
but I know I love possibility.

The Mayor says,
"Hey buddy.
Not knowing if you're in love
is like breathing in your sleep.
You don't have to realize it,
you just have to know it happens on its own.
Vote for me. I'll build you a road to Dune."

I reach to tip the waitress ghost:

"Don't try and touch the invisible, dumb ass.
That'll be twelve dollars.
Look at that wolf twitch, a-twitch twitch twitch
and he doesn't even know it.
I do that when I sleep. I didn't think I did.
My husband covered me in luminal
and videotaped me.
Just cause you don't see it
doesn't mean stuff doesn't happen."

She set down the drink and
there was nothing there.

DOWN THE I-15, I JUST HAD TO GET TO YOU

85 down the I-15,
a sparrow dropped like a rock into my windshield.

Feathers flew like every girls pillow fight.

Other cars drove through
and between the softest rock-a-bye shrapnel.

Nature splattered gorgeously on the glass of the small Japanese car.
Wings exploded from the body.

I thought of the courage it took that bird not to pull out of the dive.

I thought of the reasons.
I thought of the achievements of fear.
I thought of him just being careless.
I thought of love in your bathroom
 and drove faster.

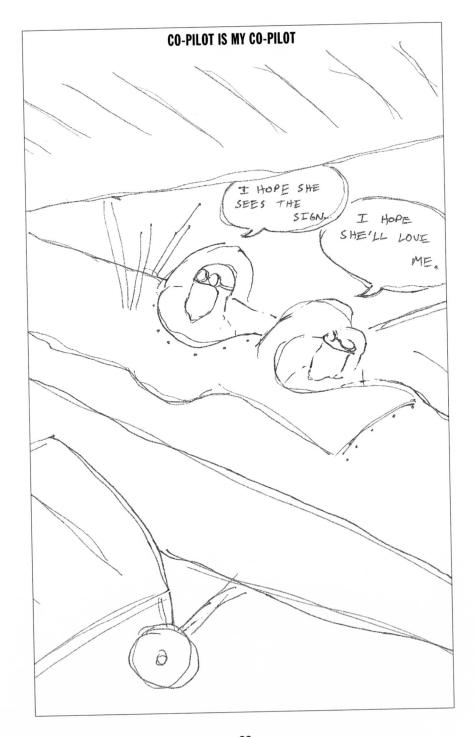

DEBBIE

Attached to a little red plane,
A sky banner floats above.
DEBBIE, DO YOU LOVE ME?

Not, Debbie I love you.
Not, Debbie will you marry me?

It detached from the back of the little red plane,
The sky banner wisping down the sky.

I WONDER WHO IT WILL LAND ON?

I imagine that person having a hell of a day
if their name happens to also be
Debbie.

SNORK IN FASHION

34

THE VALENTINE GARDEN

Everything died except for the corn.
The Tennessee clay choked most of the gifts
I was growing for her.

Beets didnt come up at all
Pumpkin stayed green and small,
Watermelon was lopsided and sour
Carrot seeds snatched in the first hour.

But the corn rose up like a boxer in slow motion.

She is from Nebraska, where
corn's abundance makes its worth to many
forgotten. To her, it was worth the feeling of home.
I wanted to remind her
of home.

I remember the night in her old apartment in Lincoln Nebraska
when I first saw her painted face.
 I froze like a child who had just
eaten a Christmas ornament.

Now we are a steady laughing during grocery shopping and slow meals at
home.

The days flow about us,
drunk snorkelers spearing
at the marine of regular living.

Nebraska wonders of other places.
It lays down in the surrounding arms of other states
and waits to have more beauty pulled from it.

Nebraska is like a rich man's house.
A home full of things you could steal
and he would never know they were gone.

We have gone regular and sometimes quiet.
The world will live without us tonight.

THE TIMING OF CAROL AND WALT

Some folks called him Dirty Walt because he never cussed.

His wife was just Carol.

I called them Grandma and Grandpa
even though we weren't blood.

Walt was a co-worker with my Father.

I mentioned his nickname at Thanksgiving once
and took a good beating for that.

I often wished I could live with the couple to see how they became one person.

I have heard of women who cohabitate
that magically link their biological clocks.
I have heard of lovers passing away at the same time.
I have heard of teammates knowing where the pass was going to go
before it was sent.

That strange power was evident in Carol and Walt.
They were connected like twins, exchanging ends of sentences.
They would take RV trips everywhere
and would sense when the other needed to stop to pee
or rummage through a thrift store.

They got sick around the same time a few years ago.
They stayed in the same hospital in Sun City.
I don't know what Walt's illness was.
Grandma Carol was fighting the mechanism in her throat.
She spoke like a broken machine.
She was tired of this non-living.

At her funeral, I remember her hands and feeling the loads of makeup.
They wheeled Grandpa Walt in.
I had never seen this icon wheeled anywhere.
They wheeled him up to the casket as the nurse held his IV.
His body was crumbling.

For me, every inch of his body was a home movie of a man cutting turkey,
a man laughing at a renegade fart,
a man swinging me in the avocado tree.

He sat hunched over emaciated and unable to form sentences.

Someone who didn't know how to control their children let their kid run up and say,
"Hi, Hi!"
The kid was laughing and patting him on the back like a little boy.
The Mother and Father oblivious.
He could not respond.
He stared into the casket the way a fisherman stares deep into a pond.

I wanted to tell the kid, "Give him some dignity."
but how do you explain that to a kid?

The nurse, trying to stop him from standing, was overpowered by his determination.

Grandpa Walt stood up, trying to disconnect his nasal tubes, pushing away the nurse.
He stood and leaned over into the gray casket and said something everyone heard.

 "I will see you soon, my love."

His wheelchair cranked as he stumbled back into it.
They knew when each other wanted to stop.

From where I was sitting, I could not see her,
but I could see the shape of the light around her.

THE BAYOU

On The Pirates Of The Carribean ride
I would step from the boat
onto the sacred world of animatronic skeletons.

I loved it because I love the secrets.

Some of my friends worked there.
I now know that the storyline of the ride
is a backward dream sequence,
with the opening Bayou scene being the modern day.

The old timer on the porch in the swamp is supposed to be
the famed pirate Lafitte, now old, spending his eternal night
watching the single shooting star on the ceiling,
scoping the two alligators with glowing eyes,
wishing he would die.

The portrait of the red-headed woman in the drunken skeleton room
is actually a portrait of the red head being sold at the auction
after she had been acclimated to the pirate lifestyle.

The useless facinates.

We go under the bridge they bring Michael Jackson across when he visits.

Of course it is scary looking.

Along the river
you can lift your hand to see where the sensors
will tell you to sit down.

When I stop hearing it,
I usually jump into the next boat or even into
a flaming basement scene. Just for a moment.
Just to be a part of the secret.

We had been drinking this time,
and not the kind the pirates do
with the spinning red ribbon in their ribs.
I closed my eyes the whole fourteen and a half minutes.
Oh Susanna played slowly in the projected clouds.

I saw
a bayou of mattresses.
People nude,
pushing themselves through the water.
I felt we were all tender
among the sludge and waste.

At the end of the ride, we took the Jackson bridge
and turned left before the door to backstage.
Sneaking behind the old man's shack.
We lurked in the swamp and watched the boats pass,
trying to bury our hiccups.

I began kissing her back into shellac.
In came the same sensation
of rolling in pink insulation,
the itching, the screee-atching.
The pollution charging my skin.

I remember her fingers extending into my hair,
channeling radio theatre into my skull.
It was a show about typing with fireworks near a bayou.

The feeling of finding her
sits on me like a gaggle of cops.

W.S. Merwin said what we look for in each other
is each other.

My woman is
cloaked in sass.

I look into her
as we hide
in a swamp of robots
and skeletons.

LISTING MY CONFLICTS WHILE DRIVING TO VALHALLA

The only thing worth writing about is the human heart
in conflict with itself.
- William Faulkner

It's OK to be nothing to everyone else
if you are everything to someone else,
especially when everyone you know keeps treating the nothing
like it was everything.

I am from everywhere I've been
and everywhere else feels like nowhere
when you are where
I am not.

There are a million living poets better than I,
but I have a million poets living inside.

I could use some religion that is in no way religious.

I like the quiet but I wasn't born quiet, I was born screaming.

The older I get, the more I like the screaming.

KVINNE

You are the ocean holding back a monsoon
from a boy on the shore.

Your spirit swirls gravity to relax the tide.
It shocks blue energy lifting waves onto the shoulders of the shore.
The way you lifted me into your hands, waiting like the cold reel of the moon.

The white wash smashes the cliffs of Huntington and screams "kvinne."
It retreats to travel past capes and islands,
past the Norwegian shores of Kristiansund
to the rocks of Trondheim
whispering "kvinne."

You are ice cream before bed,
and the holiness of an open hand stretching towards the ceiling of God.
Where is God if he is not in you?
You are a slow morning coffee
and the giggle after a spanking.

Your fingerprints float in water.
Your fingerprints float in my blood.
Your blood sloops through me at the speed of fingerprints.
Your impression left upon everything you held.

How many good things did you let go
so I could throw up in your arms all night?
  Your name shooting from my mouth like a melted record.
Me, inches from toilet death until your angels would send down Pepto Bismol.
You held me.

I don't believe you know how many nights you gave up.
You were never counting.
I was never good at math either.

Did I ever tell you how your address branded me?
When I was dropped for 20 pushups in the army
for every piece of mail received,
your address burned a smile into my triceps
and I was still weak.

Mom,
what if we were young together?
I would show you how to ride a bike fast in the street.
Riding to every public pool in all of California,
we would get kicked out for starting water fights,
riding away water-logged.
Our towels flung around the neck,
laughing at all the adults in the world.

I would challenge your wheelie all the way home.
I would hold your hand when your Mother died
and we'd sneak into the movies together,
quiet, as friends often are.

We would get old in between post cards
and I would show up at your 50th birthday party,
spilling my spiked punch
and we would laugh
and I would ask about your kids.

And you would smile a stretch of pride
within the crows of your eyes.

I would give you a bottle I found battered on an overstormed shore.
Inside it
there's the Norwegian word... kvinne.
And this word means everything.
It means woman.

THE BOX CUTTER

She has showed up to my living room
as a pile of boxes.
You are 19 brown boxes,
stacked correctly, you are a fort
and when examined closely
you have been beaten and tossed around the country
by men in short shorts.

Must I cut you to let the colors out?

I have asked these boxes to come
and crawl under the sheets with me.

Their mouths are taped shut by someone doing business.
I apologize for the business you have endured.

I touch the tan ridges and smell the dead trees
and synthetic glues of packing tape.
I lick the labels until your name and numbers splotch together.

All beautiful boxes are hiding some sort of buried offense.

Hiding deep in the packing peanuts
resting in wads of bubble wrap,
there is something awful.

I can kind of see it through the plastic stuff.
I do not touch it.

This phrase now pops in my head:
"You're healed. You're healed, now walk to me."

I wanted to make you my human,
to take off all your clothes
so I could make you more naked.

Shut up and
I'll make you naked.

Shy boxes.
I am as lost as the text for the origins of evil.
My hands move on you as sleek and aimless as a psalm.

I expect to open you and find the zippers of daylight,
or a pilot's license and a pair of keys.
Nowhere is welcome.

I lay the boxes into the shape of a robot and lay spread eagle across them.
I am with you, boxes.
Your skin beckons mailmen to marvel at your tender paper tigers.
They tear into the night to suck at your packing slips.

Your spirit rides me frantic like a junkie.
I scoop one small box into a backpack
and I head to the Hollywood Bowl.
I had to pay for two.
I spit wine into your seams.
I open you and there is only broken glass, a map and a note:

"All former lovers become blurry lessons.
All jealousy is a jail of lousy reasons.
Lay out the glass. Open the map.
Walk to me. You are healed."

CRAWLING TO THE CHORUS

Everyone on the television is laughing
at the black boy comedy.

His growth stunted by prescribed drugs,
he plays an adopted son.

I remember being nine and wanting the boy to come to my house
to make me laugh as hard as the people in the studio audience.
I wanted to be a part of a great washing body of laughter.
I wanted to know why they were laughing and if it was real.
If it was, I wanted to be there.

I wondered about the lucky black boys life.

How could he have known that while his show ran that night
and the fan mail poured in
and the money dripped down
and his family met at a Champagne fortress for the airing party,
that my mother was bleeding profusely during episode 3 season 2?

My father, hurling glass at her chest.

I was shocked at how watery blood could stream down skin.
I always saw it as corn syrup until that moment.
I wondered if it was real.
Them both screaming for demons to come out of the other.
Trying to anoint each other with oil.
Their voices escalating.

I curled up in the bathroom like a cold silkworm.
His hands pummeling like a turbine,
her hands sewing at the air,
their voices soaring like fists full of swans.
My father moving his hot ballet across her.

I could hear the neighbors closing their windows
when I finally stumbled out of the locked bathroom.

I heard their vows crawl back into the bible.

My Father sinking like a battle ship into the couch.
My Mother told me to sneak the checkbook from the kitchen and I did.
My sister and I crawled and tried to hold our breath while sobbing.
My Mother sharpened into a strength she had never known before this evening.

We piled in the Datsun and when it wouldn't start we became terrified.
Three more tries and it finally turned over.
My Father opened the garage door.
I can see him standing there with the anger gone from his eyes.

It finally started and it felt like God threw it into reverse,
a bloody exit with us in tow.

My Father just stared at us for a moment
and pressed the garage door button calmly.

I wondered if the black boy wondered about nights like this.
Revolving about is celebrity,
as he takes the sound stage,
delivering a joke someone else wrote for him
as the audience rises in laughter
like a chorus
I had dreamed

of joining.

WOMAN SLEEPING IN A ROOM FULL OF HUMMINGBIRDS

Teased by success.
We're like vampires in a tampon factory.
It doesn't have to be that way.

The only good monologue has mistakes.

I will read out of this book of drawings.
This is a book of lovers/freaks I tried to change.
I had new visions of them and tried to draw them all in a book.
The strange thing is… my drawings kind of look like you.

In some ways you look like the star of the wheelchair parade.
This one lover and I went everywhere in our wheelchairs.
I couldn't convince this lover that someday, I needed to stand on my own.
So it ended ugly and they rolled out of my life forever.

This is a self-portrait.
I drew myself as a Bengal Tiger smacked up out of its orange.
Pacing, just pacing until my next meal. Grrrr.
Shading's a little off.
I call it "Hushing my legs out to the twilight poison
of h-h-h-hot bitch knife flavored lip gloss -in still life."
This was the point in my life where I blabbed too much
and that shooed away inspiration.

I didn't have a grasp of what was happening to my heart
until after the first break up. I won't bore you with anything
but the necessary details but let's just say I was plowing anything
that smelled disinfected and didn't wear pookah shells.

I was fake.
I tried all kinds of leadership seminars
to shirk these feelings of being fake.

I started making lists to get the stripes back on the tiger.
I was watching my stripes slip from my spine,
laying there on the ground like a bunch of parentheses.
Not to sound self-righteous, but the lists became my glue to become myself again.

It was text I had crafted from a place I didn't ever know existed.
No bald headed philosophies. Just boot strap shit.

Go away therapy. Flush home pills. Make lists.
My lists started out strange.
When I got to the end of them,
I felt beautiful, but yes, they did start out strange.

#1. Do something rebellious to get out of your comfort zone.

My first graffiti art said, "Don't pierce your babies ears.
They don't like it and no one thinks it's cute except for you
and your friends with jet skis."
That felt pretty bitchin' and looked kinda gangsta in a Mormon sorta way.

#2. Write something down that is impossible and write it as possible.

It took me awhile but I came up with this little gem.

"Be on time."

There was a whole bunch I made, which are a bit embarrassing,
but the last one became my favorite.

#46. One day, when you are tired of being broken,
carefully strap little LED lights to hummingbirds,
at least 52 of them
and release the birds in your lover's bedroom at night.

When he or she asks what is going on,
tell him or her to be still,
lay there like idiots,
make some dumb wishes and enjoy your shooting stars.
The ones you made on your own.
Make endless wishes.

The birds can take it.

I'VE SEEN A HORSE FLY, I'VE SEEN A HOUSE FLY

The lady on the plane said, "Shiiiiiiit I don't' want none of these peanuts.
I want me some chicken. Shiiiiiiit! I ain't no elephant.
You know what I'm sayin'?"

I did not know what she was saying. I was busy looking at her peanuts.
I extended my long nose toward them and she said, "Oh my god, I'm sitting
next to an elephant. I didn't think elephants could fly!"

"Rarely in coach," I said.. which is a huge joke in my family
because we usually fly on private jets. I don't know if you saw Dumbo.
It was huge. That's basically my life."

MERRY CHRISTMAS YOU BUM

I once made Christmas cards for the homeless
with this girl. It was our first date.

We drew on the cards and taped money inside
with handwritten messages.

On my first card I drew a vacuum.
It said, "Sometimes Christmas sucks.
Hope this money makes you feel good."

I looked at her first card.
It said, "Sorry it's not a lot of money,
but there sure are a lot of you guys."

That seemed a bit insensitive.
Drawing a line between "us and them."

Plain felt wrong to me. I begged her to change it.
So she worked on it for twenty-eight more minutes,

And then she showed me the final product.
It said, "Sorry it's not a lot of money,
but there sure are a lot of you... people.

Merry Christmas!"

YOUR PLACE IS MINE

Sometimes sex seems like a puzzle
with two uneasy pieces.

I mixed up my birth control pills with my out of control pills.
I don't even know what you're talking about.

Sometimes sex seems as harmless as a massage on your elbow,
if your penis looked like more like an elbow. What's sex feel like to you, imagery?

Sometimes it feels like driving around with your side view mirror smashed off,
until you find your paint on someone else's car.
When you find the right person
you just want to destroy them.

I am as found in it as I am lost in it.
The easiest things to lose are your mind and your virginity
if you've got enough drink tickets.

I have four.

That is enough. How do we know if we're right for each other?
I'm not into horoscopes, but
I am into scoping whores.

The penis is a finger that doesn't realize pointing is rude.
Fingers are the new erogenous zone.
Staring at the exact place that my fingernails emerge from
I imagine how far back they go underneath the skin.
I imagine an analogy for love and trimming dead stuff.

My fingers are digits, so let me love you,
digitally.

I can't help seeing myself as a
kangaroo in a cocktail dress

with a small baby vampire in my pouch
hopping into the arms of any zookeeper
with a shiny net and a leaf.

My spine has turned to brass
and other women from the fire department
dance down me.
Money shooting from my disaster.

I've always confused love with something more meaningful.

If you love me, then you'll confuse love with sex.

ONWARD INTO THE ZIPPERS OF DAYLIGHT

She said,
They were bodies.

They were just pretty, wet bodies.

Love does not adhere to slippery men.

You can walk away from the octopus.

Tonight you are free. The scariest thing you have ever done
has left you feeling the most brave.

I have learned to speak.
I have learned that when I run, I move beautifully...
like a chandelier in a hail storm.

Step outside the octopus cloud.
The forgotten will hold you and the black will destroy you.
You might enjoy that which destroys until you are destroyed.

Leave before the numbness travels to your legs.

I am found in the forgotten.
He motions for me to stop dipping my tongue in my wounds.

Loyalty is nerdy. Loyalty is possible. Loyalty is all.

We are lovely.
We are ugly sometimes.
Good.

When the lights are out we are but wrinkles and noises.

He leans into my light and melts my candles:

"You are mathematically elegant.
You are mathematically elegant.
Wake up. I think I love you."

This dumb kite flies towards your lightning.

THE DEMONS FIRST DATE

I was so nervous.
I talked about glacial disasters and owls attacking the gray part of her eyeballs.
They were so lovely, I wanted to hard boil them.
She told me sweetness didn't sit well with her so
she puked into my glass of ox blood and it looked like clams
so we toasted:

"Here's to our brothers in heaven, may they understand why we exist. To us."

She leaned over hard and kissed my mud black tongue.
Our mouths bashed sparks like the metal salmon that charge up the river Styx.
So I jammed a fork in her eye.
She went to pierce her poison fingernails into my chest to pull out my heart
and nibble on it but as she reached into my ribs,
she pulled out... a pet rock,
which is something I usually do at parties.
I had written on it, "look up."

Molotov Cockatiels soared overhead, wings ablaze
shedding ash, which fell in the shape of cupid's arrow.
As she pulled up her eagle skin dress to defecate on it,
I felt like she could be the one.

I walked her home
tried to push her down a well
but as she lost her balance, she grabbed my warty hand
and dragged me down the hole with her.

We fell forever.

We landed in hell's sewer, which even for us, was pretty bad.
Crisp onyx crocodiles snapped at our ankles as we kicked lava puddles at
        each other.
I pretended like I was going to throw her into their path, until she ran at them,
howling like a pack of stabbed Dobermans.
She ripped their jaws clean from their heads.

She gave two to me and said, "I hope you like book ends."
I felt so... wanted, I cried kitty cat piss. I didn't even own any books,
except for a controversial one by Salman Rushdie.

The orange clouds drizzled down embers that night and she held her tongue out.
I touched her fangs and goose bumps ran down her oozing imperfect thighs.
"I care for you so much, I'd be willing to be nice for an hour.
Maybe even carry someone's groceries or not hurt children. I've never said
    that before."

I really wanted to tell her how much I hated her, but didn't want to scare her
    away.
The feeling nagged at me
as if the Anti-Christ was gestating hope in my abdomen.

 I ran my hand across her horns until she fell into a deep asleep,
so I made love to her.
I was too nervous to ask her when she was conscious.

 I touched the torch in her esophagus.
Nude, a storm of sledge hammers slid down through the thunder
and I caught one for her
 and placed it up in her womb, so she could feel like I was always with her.

I dragged her to a pile of recycled skulls
and beat one into a heart shape and she said
"What is that?"
"It's the human symbol for needing someone."
She bit into it like a Bavarian pretzel and laughed-
another damned kiss and she
 passed the white pieces into my mouth. Communion.

Wolves made of syringes followed us in wonder.
We kicked them in the needles and ran home, knocking over every
    newspaper stand
claw in claw,
as warm halcyon splashed the shores
of hell's ocean.

GOODBYE CHARLIE

Is it silly to weep for a dog that passed away?

A friends dog.

I only walked him once.

The news hit me,
a lit chimney dropped onto my kneecaps.

You can become someone's friend in an instant if the eyes are right.
Charlie and I became friends.

He had an eager madness, An ever-ready smile, and strange fur.

Charlie and I would stroll down the weedy sidewalk funk of Austin.
Stopping once to shit dead center on the path.
I pretended to fumble in my pockets for a doggie bag,
cleared my throat
and strolled away.

The low skillet of Texas concrete warmed his paws
past the scene of a UT students heads expanding and sadly, exploding
past the sound of bands discovering dissonance and a fourth chord
past the homes of stranded artists and wealthy expressionists,
We found a squirrel flirting his tail toward Charlie.

Charlie pulled at the leash and I wanted to let him go after it.

Some dogs spend their whole life pulling at the leash
And never grow tired of imagining it being gone.

It seemed as if he'd rather have the squirrel than oxygen,
the taut leash choking him some, eyes wide with instinct.

I didn't let him go.

When Jef with one F told me weeks later that Charlie,
my friend,
was dead,
I froze for a bit.

Gone already?

How can I be paralyzed by the death of one animal
when news reports of the human dead
and the near dead surround me.

The answer was morose.
It is hard for me to care for what I have never known.
I can't picture their faces alive.
I can't imagine their favorite movie.
I can't imagine their inability to match socks.

I hope Jef, you know I am grateful
 to have known Charlie.

I pray that maybe someday
 you will see his passing
as a pure exit,
as pure
as scissors
to a leash.

I FEEL SAFE WHEN YOU LIE

In somno securitas.

She slid into bed
easy as a knitting needle
into the spine of a hare.

I threw a bag of chalk into the air
across her body
while she slept.

I lit black lights into action
                    watched the frenzied prints emerge
from her breasts, neck, and thighs,
souvenirs of desire.

I breathed across her tight sandtan stomach.
Chalk dust blew into her nose and she awoke.

I asked her
if the man made love to her with all his might?
Did it feel the same?
Did his beads of sweat fall upon the necklace I worked for?
Did he extend the milky antennae of her legs into the air?
Did you tune in God on the meat hook channel?

She said
"My dear
slow jealous detective,
come sleep by me.
These prints are yours
and always yours,
they simply will not wash away.
You have had your head in other people's hands
for so long
you forgot what your own touch looked like."

The faders of twilight approached.
I curled into her with my arms
dead across her ribs
feeling the rate of her heartbeat increase
as she wonders
if I can feel a lie
through her nightgown.

It is the feeling I get
when ice skating
through the rising crackles of sunshine.

In sleep there is safety.

HOW DID I BECOME A DAMNED CARTOON?

It sounded like a good idea at the time. Helping kids, right? Helping blind kids on Easter looks good on paper. My buddy Buzzy said to me, "We're doing this benefit day for the blind children's center of Orange County. We need someone to be the bunny. You like kids. You seem kinda motherly. It's for a good cause. Why not give it a shot?"

If someone ever asks you to be in a bunny suit for blind children, I recommend that you don't do it. Someone is gonna get hurt. In the face. And it will be a small Mexican child.

I should've realized that most of these kids would be picnicking outdoors with food smashed all over their blind faces. Luckily Easter this year fell on a smoldering weekend and I was the dope cooking in the furry suit. I was so soaked in sweat,
I thought my underwear was crying.

I could hardly see out the huge rabbit head. Are huge heads still funny to people? Are bobble heads flying off the shelves? Does anyone say, "Look, it's funny cause it has a big head?"

But here I am in 90 degree heat with a basket full of eggs in a suit made of carpet and lead trying to trick kids who have never seen a rabbit into thinking I am a rabbit that is as tall as a human and has bad taste in multi-colored vests. If I was a real rabbit this big, I'm sure I'd be as timid as most rabbits, but my shit would be more outstanding and duplicitous. And why would I wear a vest with no pants to a child's party? I'm going to send a letter to Winnie the Pooh.
At the park, I struggled to leave my friends VW bug and finally we walked holding hands to the picnic tables full of kids. The Easter Bunny is supposed to be a dude and I doubt he holds hands with anyone in his sad egg shaped home. Buzzy yelled out: "Hey everybody, the Easter bunny is here!"

Silence. No reaction. Not one yelp.

Buzzy whispered to me, "Oh man, we got deaf and blind kids. You're gonna have to really turn it up a notch. If they get restless, just give 'em some more candy and that should calm 'em down." Which as all Moms will tell you, is ridiculous.

A woman walked up to Buzzy and said "Hey Buzz. Thank you guys so much for coming. This means a lot to us. These groups of kids have been blind since birth. You'll have to explain to them what an Easter bunny actually is. I'm sure they'll love you."

Buzzy confidently nodded at her; "I think it would be better if the Easter bunny explained himself to the kids, one on one." I spun my constantly erect ears toward him. He just motioned with his elbow for me to go to the kids who were snacking on hot dogs and coke. I stood there for about 30 seconds, looking back at him, unsure of how I got in this position and I began seriously pondering what cities I could move to so I could get some decent friends who think that torture is something you reserve for your enemies.

I tried to wipe the sweat from my forehead, but actually ended up wiping the rabbit's furry head with my glove. I cleared my throat.
"Hey kids. My name is... the Easter bunny."

One kid lifted his head up towards me but did not look at me.

"Your name is the Easter bunny?"

"What? Yes. I am the Easter bunny... and my name is the Easter bunny. I am a rabbit... who can talk. It is Easter so I've brought you all some eggs. Some are painted. Some have toys or sweets in the eggs... that I squatted and gave birth to."

Buzzy elbowed me on that one. He then guided me to a bench and gathered the un-amused children around me. I don't know how well they could hear me in that muffled suit.

"Is this a jacket? This feels like a jacket or a rug for the bathroom," said one of the eight year olds as he ran his hands down the front of my costume.

"Are you here 'cause of Jesus?" asked a smaller kid.

"Aren't we all?" I replied.

An older kid piped up, "No. I'm not here cause of Jesus. I'm here cause of my Mommy and Daddy made me. Jesus didn't make me. Jesus only saved me from hell."

"I know. Would you like an egg with a jellybean in it?"

Now all these hands were all over me as one of my paws instinctually moved to protect my breasts. I felt like Braille. I felt like Bugs Bunny at a mustang ranch for pedophiles. They were asking questions one on top of the other and weren't waiting for me to respond;

"Why are you wearing that?"
"Can I have more candy?"
"Are you supposed to be a dog or a monster?"

I interrupted to get their hands off of me.
"Hey you guys want to play helicopter? Follow me."

I hopped off toward an open area wondering if any of these kids actually wanted to play in this heat. Three kids tried to run and follow me. One ran into a metal garbage can, which always sounds worse than it feels. One girl got clothes lined by a badminton net. And one lone six-year-old Mexican kid named Miguel made it to me. He stuck his arms out and just put one hand on me, just to make sure I wasn't going away. As volunteers tended to the injured, I asked the kid,

"Would you mind if I took off my headpiece, just for a little bit. Would that freak you out? I'm really burning up in here."

"What headpiece?" said Miguel.

"I'm wearing this rabbit costume and I have this mask on and it sucks. I don't think anyone cares or thinks I'm actually a rabbit, I don't think anyone knows what Easter has to do with bunnies and plastic eggs or the catholic church and druids, so if you wouldn't mind, I'd at least like to take off the mask for a bit. I'm seriously cooking in this bitch."

The kid looked off toward the street. "Sure. I don't care. I just want someone to play with. We can be friends today."

I grabbed the sweet little bastard's hands with my paws and began to spin him in a circle until his legs lifted off into the air. With his arms outstretched and spinning faster, Miguel actually squealed a little.

"Heeee. I'm flying. I'm flying. The rabbit is making me fly! Look at me everybody. Look at me! I feel like I'm flying."

The saddest looking kid of the bunch was laughing his head off. I felt good. I felt like a good person. So that's what it's like. All of a sudden I felt un-ri-diculous. All the pain that this volunteering had led to had become worth it. I gave some kids some jellybeans and made a few kids laugh. There is some-thing for me to learn from every person's story. I thought maybe, if my life is built on suffering a little bit every day so…

And then my paw-gloves slipped off my sweaty hands and Miguel went flying across the grass until he landed in a spread eagle belly flop by the sprinklers. He ended up getting the wind knocked out of him hard. Miguel lifted his little wet grassy face up, crying.

I stared at him, frozen, like I broke him.

They took him into the shade and I waited for him to stop weeping. Buzzy explained to the workers what happened.

"Are you O.K. Miguel? I am so, so, so sorry."

"It's O.K. Easter bunny. I would like to do it again, but my ribs hurt."

"You're a tough guy Miguel. I would like to give you my mask, so you remem-ber me."

Buzzy whispered in my ear, "You can't. It's a rental."

"Miguel, I would like to give you this colorful basket. You can put things in it."

"Thank you Easter bunny. I will put things in it, maybe today it will be a hot dog."

Miguel gave me a hug, told me I was sweaty. He said he couldn't wait for me to come back. I told him that next time he loses a tooth, I would sneak into his bedroom and beat that tooth fairy down with my lucky feet and then we could hang out as friends, when it's not so damn hot out.

THE ELEPHANTS ARE HER SLAVES

1.
I came to your blood hole.
Dressed up like Mastodon.

Your tar pits
were full of white girls
who wished they were black.

2.
An epileptic in a restaurant
rejected my help once.
He said it been happening all his life
and that I should leave him alone.
He continued to tremble and drool
reaching for the support of the table.

You asked if I was going to turn that into a metaphor.
I just turned out the lights and went to black.

3.
You sprint to all trauma.

4.
Your throat is plugged into every siren

5.
Relax, you're gay.

6.
Was not a very good line. I cut it. Slave stuff.

7.
I would rather have 400 great nights of power
and die at 35
than have only 6
and die at 82.

8.
Raise the murder sails.

9.
Teach children the good lust.

10.
Laugh into blood holes.

11.
Tell her the breasts are built on a hollow foundation.

12.
Unplush your hospitals

13.
Set wet stars to shine.

14.
Learn the melody found at the end of a whip.

HOW THE JELLYFISH WISHES

The farmer's boy was born in a season of drought
and dreamed nightly of the western coastline
where it was rumored
that all the stars were migrating
to crash into the sea.

No one knew why this was happening to the stars, it just was.

He awoke with his body in the soft L shape of California
and began to pack.

He was through spending his life between harvesting sweat
and day-gazing upon the scalp of the horizon
for something that felt like home.

He grew up working the soil
and understood that he was like a crop,
that he was just a patch of minerals that rose from the earth
and demanded water.
Crops are based in seasons and transformation.
A life,
no different.

Corn was a maze his family had been lost in
for generations.
Some years it was beans.

"Everything changes in this farm but us.
Starlight has stopped visiting. I am going West to join it."

He would be the first to seek
the visions of streaking light spittering brightly
into the endless onyx arms
of the Pacific.

By dawn, he would not look back.

Orange buckets of light spilled a rusted dusk
across the maple and oaks of Tennessee.

The fields along his route
sizzled with the chamber music of cicadas and bullfrogs.
Possums went squinting at the cackled dawn.
Endless fences poked up like bad teeth
in the sunlit mouth
of a fallen giant.

He raced away on a lazy train with eighty dollars crumpled
and a journal.

Lightning had slammed its brights on outside
as he skimmed earlier entries:

"None of the teachers could explain why
The stars were migrating west.
The word on the street was that some states had fell
into a season of mental drought,
where people stopped moving their beds near windows.

They settled into dreaming of bills, tanning salon gift cards
and affordable karate practice.
They stopped wishing.
There was no work for stars here."

When he reached the sea he found headlines in the L.A Times
stating that the stars had come to light the sea.

They looked like lighthouses being flung into the deep.

So now the sea finally had its chance to wish:

How do we know this came to pass?

Have you heard of fish that wish for wings near Avalon harbor?
You can watch them lift into aerials like fat finches.
Have you heard of diatoms that wish for their remains not to be scattered
but to be used in dynamite and toothpaste?
Have you heard of turtles wishing to live longer
so they can nap with their children just a few hundred more years?
The jellyfish wish their hearts to become luminescent.
The eight-armed writers wish to shoot ink at their enemies.
Some bland fish wish for only the skin of a rainbow.
Have you heard of the humpbacks who wish for the ability to sing for 10 hours
straight to serenade their families swimming home to the sound of their voice?
Tiny creatures, tired of their fins, asking to become horses of the sea and
they got it.
They all got it
because they asked.
Because they don't know what silly is.

The farmers boy always wished he could sing.
He dove in.

You could see him underwater.
You could see everything around him.

THE PROFESSIONAL DRINKERS OF CALGARY, CANADA

Calgary had a rodeo, private booze holes
and a job for me in a plastics factory
that paid twice as much as delivering ergonomic floor mats
to people who never looked me in the eyes.

So I'm here.

It as a good place to die
from freezing your ass off.

I live in a house unknown.

I've settled into a mausoleum of lonely drunks.
They're coming in out of the cold like stiff snow angels
clocking out from working the ice mines.

Calgary's famed drinking brigade bobs in parade unison
under street lights that fight to shine in sallow air.

Crunch, Crunch, Breath fog. Crunch.

Shirts tucked deep to the last testicles crinkle.

Some of us wouldn't know what to do with drinking buddies
if we had them.
I know everyone as much as I can.

I've seen the guy in the red and black flannel for 4 years and I don't know
        his name.
I wonder why no one says it or even 'buddy' or 'hey man.'
I know his beard gets filthier and funnier every month.
I know the owner shakes the ice from his boots longer than anyone.
The two women in the corner are fat and ride snowmobiles while wearing
        racing helmets.
I can't imagine them going fast,
without imagining them sliding on their bellies down glaciers.

That's what they get for wearing white turtlenecks with black ski bibs.

A young man that walks to the bar from work
once talked to me about eating moose,
and how it seemed less humane to eat a moose.

I agreed with him but I didn't know why.

I know the old man in the mustard overalls drinks
like he never wants to go home.
I would like to get to know him.
To tell him I don't have much to say,
that I could use a double for every minute I try to figure out
which question I really want to ask:

why I am alive or why I'm not dead.

The TV by the pickles plays the sound of people turning
to the colors of old city snow.

Crunch. Crunch.

PORTRAIT OF AN ARTIST REACHING FOR THE THING

All your aimless jazz is done.

Tonight you must become.

Stop yelling at the movie screen.
You know the screen needs tenderness.

You're an absolute genius if you stole a TV
to protest the treatment of Blacks by the LAPD during the riots.
You should steal my car to end genocide.
Punch me in the face to end racial profiling.
Stab a Shetland pony to get DJ's to start playing music they actually like,
anything to keep from the danger pains of dialogue.

Do you want to kill?

Kill music television for not playing music on the television.

And please tell hip hop I am tired of being told that all the people say Ho
because they don't. I don't.
Not even around Christmas time
And yes, the party is over there.
The killing is over here.

Please tell rock and roll to stop moping.
I'll be the first to say it... annunciation is cool.
Look me in the eyes is cool. Not too much.

Why don't you unfold your arms at this living concert?

Kill the subscription.

How can you lust for those dead-eyed models?
Stop visualizing them glorifying your National Monument.
Visualize (them) wiping their ass after a nasty beer turd
and they won't seem more special than you
anymore.

Killers going in!

Shhh.
In my bed, someone's hands are cackling antlers together.
It's kill kill season.
I tell the killers
that hunting anything with an assault weapon,
makes you a sissy.

You can start a war with a pen.
You can end it too.

I propose a toast to the breadless.

When we drink
we are friends
if you drink
like it's all going to end.

We will march home
swallow the yellow fuzz of streetlights,
stare in the mirrors at ourselves
wait for the bastard to emerge and say:

Am I an artist?
Am I closer to the thing?
I can't get the thing.

I want the thing
but, I can't get it.

It's the thing I want.
In the morning
wake up fresh for the kill
and just begin. Everything you want to do:

You only must begin.

EATING THE HULL

A man in Texas and I discussed our most favorite feeling we can remember.
I think I mentioned a kite and some wine
or a sailboat dinner.

He asked me what sailboats tasted like
and I didn't get it at first.

He talked about a time
when he worked at a sandwich shop and had to make the condiments
and on Fridays he would fill a surgical glove
with guacamole
and slide his hand in it
when no one was looking,
opening and closing his fist through the green thickness.

He made an Ooh Ahh Oooh Ahh sound.

I asked him if he ever got lonely.

He said, "Never."

ODE TO THE ROCK ACTION

Speech I gave to the crowd on behalf of musical artist Jay Buchanan at the Exit In,
Nashville when he opened up for pop star Ryan Cabrera
to a crowd of screaming 14 year old girls, 2006

Ladies, perverts, industry people that came in here smelling like money.
and children of all ages,
Have you ever had a dream burst from the ass of a Pegasus?
Have you ever broke a sweat on the inside, Ladies?
Have you ever had the gunpowder in the 'never tan' area of your panties
ignite into the bright lust of rock action?
Get ready for some music that will make you even more virgin
when the purist voice rings out and asks,
"Have you too, ever felt that empty feeling
and you're not sure if you need the Lord
or a ham sandwich?"
Maybe you just came in here tonight lost and looking for love...
Put away your compass Dora, because you've just been found,
by the international leg spreader known as _____.
God Bless.

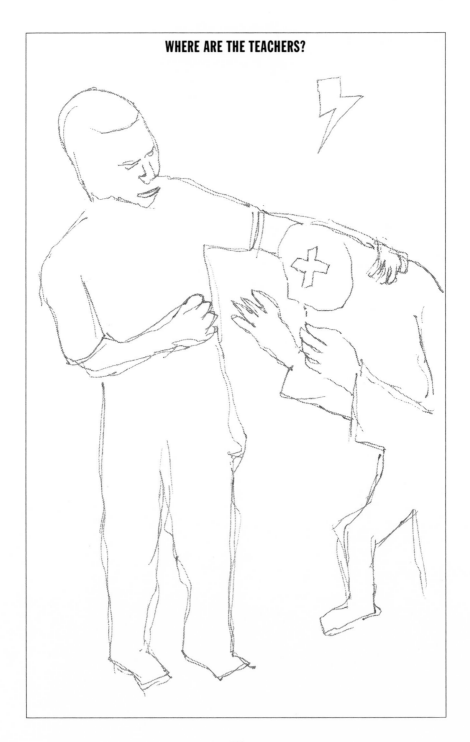

THE VICTORY EXPLOSIONS

I try to remember my youth.
It evaporates into 76 memories.

One memory was that you believed
the earth was made perfect by God,
and that humans fouled it up
and that sin was something we gave birth to,
as God shook his head at our idiocy.
"How could they choose terror and loss?"

I don't think God really ever wanted perfection
if he designed the things he made with an instinct to screw up.

Fighting it and sometimes failing is beautiful and hard.
Screwing up is part of the program. Call it sin. Call it human.
Maybe there are codes built inside of darkness needing light
and vice versa.
 It did not shake your belief in the existence of a God,
but it shook your belief in the bland necessity for perfection.

It birthed the belief that
the human who could figure out
the balance of a hunger for winning and a deep respect for losing
would win the life trophy.

You go back to the first year you learned to daydream in a clothing rack.
The first year butterflies bloomed adrenalized
in your wet guts.
In the 5th grade you tempted everything.
Bicycles spinning,
the smell of girls,
pencils at war,
dismantled radios.

Launching off the swing set into the air, your first sensation of flight.
An innocent season for getting your ass kicked by a boy
who thought it would be a nice sign of his love.

Adam White heard I'd kissed her underwater at her Dutch pool party, French
    style, which is weird for a 5th grader.
These were skill sets as a 5th grader; my tongue was not prepared for.
I did not know who started the rumor,
but I was about to pay for it with the cash of my face.

The same field we chased girls together in,
the strong, freckled Adam challenged me to my first fistfight.
I felt like a coward in a costume of a coward.
I was skinnier than a dead model.

 No matter how much I denied the rumor,
his freckles kept popping from his face like brail.
"You're ass is grass, Derrick Brown."

I know.

The crowd gathered.
I stared at them like a sparrow
trapped in an airport terminal,
wanting the sky but stuck against the glass.

I stood like a cricket in a junkyard of fiddles
unable to stop my legs from shaking music from my knees.

He swore he loved her, and that I would pay.
His forehead blistering
wrinkling like a crumpled valentine.

Where in the hell were the teachers?
What I wanted was mercy.
But even I didn't know what that word meant.

His fist came out and crushed at my jaw.
My eyes went black and all that I saw
was a shower of lighting bugs.
Children flashing into sunshine.
My teeth penetrating my cheek.
 Falling backwards,
blood fertilizing the softball field.

But instead of freezing, I stood up again.
He struck me down, once more.
Eyes, ricocheting against the back of my skull.
The earth, meeting my failure, legs buckling,
skin reeking with contact,
and I stood up again.

And he socked me with all his might.
 Matchsticks lighting in my cheeks.

And I stood up again.

And he hit me so hard my Mother's eyes bled.
And I fell again, and I stood up again, and again, and again, and again,
until he grew tired of socking me and left. Everyone left.

Alone there, baptized in warm blood,
I now knew the cost of the satin sponge and slop of a girls ridiculous lips.
Cause guess what?
We did kiss under water at that Dutch pool party
like aqua spies
and it was worth it.

There's nothing for me to learn from winning.

It is losing that has yielded the unforgettable lessons.

Losing is pregnant with chance.
Victory escorts loss to every dance.

Harmony,
harmony.

THE LAST POEM ABOUT ANNE SEXTON

There must have been a moment when she thought
about the photo of her daughter
on the hallway mantle.

The kid.

Listening to the car gargle in that swampy garage.
The door locked.

Garden hose crammed up the cunt of the exhaust pipe.
Sitting there in the drunken shade of irreversible.

All the film negatives in the house of family photos,
melting.

To know that she had to choose and to know what she chose
makes me wonder about people.

It makes me wonder if her daughter can get up off her knees.
Not clench her teeth every time she holds a hose.
Watering the lilies,
hoping next year's annuals will last longer than this.

This came to me in a sweat and kept me up.

The way Jesus stayed up
the night he saw how
he was going home.

OSIRIS IN PIECES

I share things with strangers
I could never share with my Mother.

"That thing I dreamed of may never occur."

A Banshee orchestra is trying to play gently.

I hear the goose wings played
soft
ly
and the lingering
gray
sighs
of loneliness.

Songs telling me of all the things I should've pulled off.
I get sad.

People go to pieces.

Some people get re-assembled as more powerful mummies.
Some don't.

I can sigh my way into love
and I can pummel my way out.

It is not that.

I can't even tell you.

SOUTH SIDE IRISH FESTIVAL

The girls on the floats were tossing Bushmills Whiskey necklaces to the kids.

This is Chicago. Even the kids are tough.

We stood on 108th and western in 2 _ hours of beer.

Joel's girlfriend played the bagpipes by tapping on her throat. Of course they
    are in love.

When we saw the water reclamation team on their float we all started chanting,
"Take it back!"

When the immigrant awareness league came by, we began to chant,
"Put Ellis island on Lake Michigan where it belongs!"

 I saw a woman's genitals, trying to pee behind a plastic sheet.
Her boyfriend said "At least buckle up, ya kooze, what a slag."

The Monaghan family was sad,
marched embarrassed.
Floats full of non-dancing Celtic dancers make you want to get up there
and just spaz the hell out.

 Joel, in his Referee shirt, I in my Viking cap and turtle Shalaleigh settled down
for a short winters collapse.

On the Special Olympics float, I showed a girl my white sox jersey and she smiled.
She raised her gold medal over her neck and blew me a kiss.
 It landed on Joel's fake Ditka mustache.

Saint Patrick came by passing out beads.
An old man next to me didn't get any,
and yelled, "Up yours saint Patrick! It's O.K., I'm Catholic."

We walked along the train tracks to 97th street and drank Jameson out of
    someone's necklace.

Joel threw a rock at a train passing at 40mph. It ricocheted squarely into my
    left bicep. When you're drunk, pain becomes funny.

CBS2 news came by. I yelled in their microphone, "I love your weather man
to the max," I didn't know who he was, but I bet it was the only weatherman
shout out in the History of Chicagoland news.

We make it to some kind of bar.
We all sit and laugh and wait for our holiday.

Each stranger in the bar feeling like they had found family.
The kind of family that you don't have to say anything to
you just know,
the kind of family
that might
barf on you

when you're not looking.

NICE CAREER MOVE

Fingers hit her skin
like rain into tundra.

Snowbox,
My snowbox,
You are not above chiseling madness.

Ice sculpture
with your thighs.

You can have the unborn kids.
I'll take the evening without a gown.

My life is business now.
I give my devotion to the company.
I live forced
into a tiny suit.

I turn to the arms of the city.

Skylights wept glass upon me.

I tried to catch it on my tongue
so I could blood dial you
in the middle of the night.

You would not understand a word.

AMATEUR REALIST, ASCENDING

For Daniel McGinn.

In the dead locomotive colors of night you're at the bottom of the dark staircase.
Gazing at the tired soldiers you just tucked in.

You wonder about your wife.
Smile as she hovers lovely,
the way angels do when they fear the thought
of landing in lakes.

You wonder about the honor of your sons
and the necessity of money.

You wonder where they got the notion to prank you in your sleep
with wet rags on your ankles.
Tickling your nostrils after loading shaving cream piles
in both your hands.

The glowing under your shirt that you noticed at work after your boys had
    secretly built a lighthouse in your sternum…
Complete with 2-inch Scottish watchman,
guess where that came from.

Freckles, blue pants, a life laughing 'til near suffocation.

Let her guide you home
to the one with arms shaped like roman candles.
You unscrew a fingernail and pour out the day's matchsticks upon her.

You write with one hand on the page
and one hand in the candle's flame.

The hair on your arms melt into fuses.
The Wilco and smoke asserts itself over your body.
You fall asleep like a love letter under the bed.

The ceremony continues
as the lion tamer slips into his savior pajamas.
Tamed by the lighthouse, tamed by her hair that falls upon him
like rock and roll.

What I know of you
I hope to become.

ALL LOST IN THE SUPERMARKET

At the supermarket
an employee had taken the stock photography from the picture frame
and put a slightly blurry picture of his garage rock band in it.

I wanted to tell the scraggly mom in the frozen section.
I wandered the market and couldn't get myself to speak to anyone.
It seemed like such a tiny 'screw you'
 that only the employee would know about,
but I had noticed and felt good.

I guess I love to look at the stock pictures in new frames
and wonder why most photographers try to make the world look well lit.

I wandered through the pet food and wished for dogs to leap out of the bags.

I don't know why I didn't have the guts to open my mouth to anyone
about something that wasn't gutsy at all.
I just wanted someone to also see it and smile,
and look at me like we were winning.

This was like swimming alone
at Fall Creek Falls in August
and all you wanted was a woman with you
who knew how to talk about water crashing
but says nothing
and instead
does something with her hands
that makes you feel baptized
in blood.

BAR LUCK

Los Angeles is a wound you can live in.

She is varnished trash doused in platinum.
She is spread eagle in neon action.
She is spitting re-invention into the mouths of the unknown.
She is a cold cadaver you still caress.
Each high rise at night is a necrophiliac's finger on a black girl's wig.
She waits like a widows panties,
and is as understood as expensive silk
on an Otter's balls.

On Sunset and Hillhurst there is a bar called Bar Luck or something.
The interior glows in soft oriental red.
Shadows bounce across vinyl booths.
All the leather jackets have been Xeroxed and distributed.
Some poor, poor man has to wear sunglasses inside.

The waitress swallows the music in her dress.
She obeys the 51% law. It is the law of erotica.
When getting dressed, you should try to not show more than 51% of your body.
Have you heard of this law? You have?
I just made it up.

There are mirrors on the walls to see who is seeing whom.
I heard a New Yorker talk about how much they hated LA.
I leaned over and told her to stop whining
and that it is wonderful and shitty everywhere.

The truth is that everywhere I haven't been
always
seems more wonderful than where I am.

She said to me as I was leaving, "Are you going to go have fun somewhere else?"
I said, "There's too many people out tonight."
She said "Thursday is the new Saturday."
I said "Friday is the new Christmas. You missed Chanukah."

I am not Jewish.

I closed out with the waitress.
She said, "You're lucky. I wish I could go home. But I gotta make the big bucks."
I said, "I wish you could go home.
I wish you could go to my home so you can make me peanut butter treats.
Then I would make you think I was going to cut you with a broken mirror
but really I would just be trying to get on top of you to show you how good
your eyes made me feel."

I accidentally walked the wrong way to my car.

I wonder if there's some metaphor in getting lost
in a town you love,
that doesn't love you back.

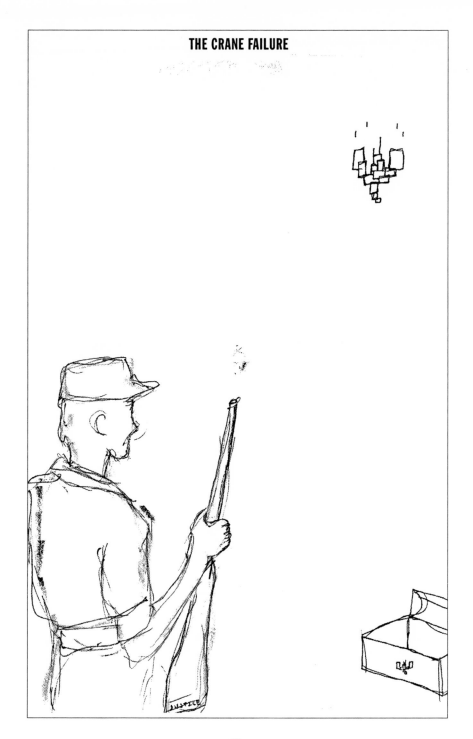

VIRGIN GOSPEL

At a watering hole full of lying virgins
he passes me a lukewarm
cheese on a stick and says, "That
is a bona-fide hot piece of ass.
But I guarantee you this: someone,
somewhere
is tired of boning her."

Scott has a voice like a driveway.
I have a nude hunger for barroom gospel.

 "I was a son of a bitch to someone."
He knows I know it
and appreciates the concept of forgiveness from a 3rd party.

We discuss the fact that no one has record of Judas as a boy.
Perhaps he wanted nothing more than to collect figs in the summer
and to make his mother proud.

What a twist.

As he passes his drink for me to sample,
a woman steps from a magazine with an ass
like an impala.

He says, "You ever hit something beautiful like that?"

I rubbed my eyes so hard, there were lights.

The first thing that pops in my head
is the time, as a child, I shot a crane out of the Texas sky.

I thought we would eat it, but you can't.

Running to the limp white death
in the coastal Bermuda grass—
I stood there
watching its life flicker.

A thing of beauty
choking under my shadow.
The bird breathed itself out,
flittering frightened wings,
trying to fly back into the light.

A kid named Benji finished it off with a shotgun to the head.

"Well, have you?" Scott says.

"Yes," I say, "And it felt good."

I JUST WASTED A MINUTE OF YOUR LIFE

In the red swells of Arizona
there is a national monument called
"The Early Man Site."

When you get to the end
of the dark cavern
there's a man in a suit that says,

"Dude, I've been here since 6 AM. Where's my scone?"

DROP ZONE

A paratroopers ballad.

They jumped us into a cold and wet North Carolina drop zone one night. I can still hear the freezing sound that a Southern forest coughs out when you are a few hundred feet above it.

Twelve airborne artillery soldiers fell silently from a C-141. We landed off our mark and were lost in the dark sludge of somewhere. I found a flower in that endless drizzle of brown and black.

From the full moonlight I could see it was a brittle yellow dahlia's with a long two-foot stem.

How does anything last in weather like this? It didn't smell like anything. It couldn't overpower the steady rank of damp clothes and gun oil.

Our squad paused nearby and I snapped one down to six inches and stuck it in my helmet, to take it into the morning, as if I was rescuing it from the dark.

We thought the advance party team was going to meet us and that they would take us home to the barracks. They never showed. Sarge told us we were gonna march. I told him that would fuck us if the AP was on its way, and we should wait for a red flare. He slapped me like Steve said he slaps his Korean wife.

We marched for so long my head began to tingle. We marched right into a stream and we stood there while Sarge fumbled around through his bag of leadership skills.

A white flare went up into the sky.

This was a way to spot the enemy for a beginning artillery barrage. We knew we could be in the line of fire with no communication and we would die right here if we didn't get away from the hot spots. We took cover in the stream, poised, water up to our titties. Two cherries moaned and shivered. Sarge told them it was demoralizing to hear their teeth chattering and threatened them with necessary dental work after a severe pummeling. They couldn't help it. When your teeth chatter and your body shivers uncontrollably you are exhausted and it just makes you chatter more. Infuriated, he dunked them both in an unnamed stream.

I pulled the privates to shore. Sarge pushed me aside and scorched them with a whisper; "You two cherry homosexuals want to ruin this mission? You should've joined the Peace Corps, you California Cockgobblers. Only two things come out of California: Fast cars and faggots and I don't see no tail pipes coming out of you. Pussyass bitches. Next time you compromise our position, I will end you! You wanna fuck me? You wanna ruin me, faggot? You wanna see how sweet I am?"

A large object, maybe an M203 barrel, crashed down on the back of Sarge's helmet. Our Kevlar helmets were loose enough to see a few stars if someone gave it a good smack with their hand. I didn't do it. I was glad someone did.

It snapped his head forward into a tree limb and he fell unconscious. Shaw launched an emergency sequence of two white flares in a row. A knock to the helmet would normally only send someone to the earth, but we were all dead tired and that limb got him good.

We threw our ponchos around the heap of man on the ground. You know when you're a kid and you are playing "let's make dinner" in the backyard and the burritos are really just leaves wrapped around dirt clods? That's what he looked like. Fitz and I went for help. We found the advance party making their way to where our flares had released. We told them Sarge had passed out due to FDP. "FDP?", they asked. "Faulty depth perception. He's got it bad. I've seen him hold a chicken nugget in front of his face and just take a big ol' bite of air. It's creepy."

Sarge then became semi-conscious and was mumbling: "Cherries, God damn cherries...Corvettes...Corvettes are made in Kentucky...what the fuck."

They asked us why there was a flower in his helmet band. I told them. "I'm not sure," I said, "I heard he was from California but I don't see no tail pipes."

I took the Dahlia from his helmet as they carried him off. We followed in staggered formation close behind and I wanted to place the flower back in the woods. But it was dead now... or it was already dead when I found it and the petals, defiantly, refused to give up its color.

I kept it to remind me.

THE EGG

Were you born
blank as an egg?

Or did the gray sparkplug in your head crank on early?

Before inception. In silence.

You, as a blob-fant
fought to hold onto that "I'm home" feeling of tiny swimming.
You fought to remember the melodic horror,
the stretching of your new flesh-
all erased upon intake of oxygen and ripping.

It came back to you, thirty three years later.
You are remembering what you lost at birth.

The possibilities found in silence.

You were silence before oxygen... then...
You were born
and you were noise.
and you were music.

At the first portions of light you saw something but you just couldn't remember it
You just couldn't speak

Something grew inside your mouth, simultaneous with you mind
and it allowed you the ability to make music with your breath
and tongue shapes
and soon others understood this music and you understood theirs,
some of theirs.

The music became everything.
Shocked full of the shanks of hate or steadily fading like the flashbulbs of love.
Darker definitions of time.
Necessary solitude,
math as a path to God
and comedy united with fear.

You found a need for music inside.
You were pressing your hands to paper,
nothing came out.

There was a new voice buried inside your pubis.
It sounded like a woman cursing that silence you came from,
mocking your hometown.

And she handed you a pen
and you moved your hands across paper and made shapes with the pen
made the counsel laugh and cry.

From here on, there would be no more silence.
There would be the shape of:

Sin as path to more glamorous churches
Horror as a sedative in your popcorn
Insanity as a trapdoor to genius and shitmagnets
Terror as a ghost that wants blood over victory
Moral pressure in your bike tires
Altruism as an advertising slogan
Guilt as a way to end humanity
Nascent language as a path to blowjobs
Exoneration as a new spelling for whoops
Tits as an unlearned mystery
Seeing your cock as a friend of a friend

Where are you going?
You're going to get it out.
There's an AM radio in the fillings of your teeth.

The pages are bleached
 -calling to you-
the you that was as blank as an egg.

Turn back.

YE OLDE HERMITAGE OF POWER

I was real thirsty,
 I went into a Saloon.

All they did was cut my hair, shampoo and blowdry it.

One missing O from the word saloon can ruin your day.

I went to a local hermit's house to cheer up.

His hermitage.

He had a sculpture garden of famous sculptures.
He had a sign that said, "Don't sweat the petty things
and don't pet the sweaty things."

He was nuts and bright in a suit of white.

I liked his cabin.
The paint was peeling from him singing off key into it.
He had lined the ice cube trays with pancake syrup for breakfast parties.
He had a sketchbook of over 300 drawings of hands.
 I said what is this? He said, for me, it's ESL pornography.

He said he once saw a catholic mime cussing,
and he told the mime to wash his hands 12 times.
I said I know how he felt cause I caught a vegetarian eating animal crackers.
Yes, we argued about conviction.

He leaned into my earlobe: "Let's talk the real deal.
If man evolved from apes, why are there still apes?"
I asked him if he ever saw a Latvian with his shirt off. No reply.
That ended the ape conversation.

I asked him "How do you feel out here, nothing happening, all the time."
He said it suits him. He told me his parents fornicated in a manger
and then chilled for years, waiting for good to fall into their laps.
Nothing Jesusy happened. They died waiting. Their tombstones were
slot machines that reads WE LOSE when you hit three stars.

He misses the North Star when the earth turns its' back.
He once tried to chase the meaning of life
and just ran out of breath.

He is differential.
Now, he never says 'Hey' when he really means, "Hi, I missed you sssss much."

I told him he left the O out of so. He said we have a lot to learn from each other,
especially by looking at what we don't say.

He then took a machete to a dictionary and told me
that a dictionary was an authors photo album of their kids
and that kids don't need to make sense all the time.
They just need you to be there.

I asked him why he was chopping 'em up.

He said, "fiddle diddle squid.
Bronze aggression
Antwerp summer
Camera Belgium pantyhose
Snowman posse
Fuzzy party bolts
disco ball chance
tornado sweat pounce
hamstring Paducah!

There is a lot to learn
in a hermitage.

SECRETS OF EUROPE

Joel said, "I can't believe these toilets here in Europe.
They let your moist poop chill just 4 inches from your butt
with no water to kill the stank.
It just sits there piling up right there, like bad Lincoln Logs,
close to your ass."

"I guess people here aren't afraid of the ugly side of being human," I said,
"They can examine it and maybe some actually enjoy being close to it."

He said, "Oooh Captain Stack-ums.
Maybe your ass could learn the secrets of the pyramids!"

Soon we were engaged in a hip hop rap battle outside of a bar in England.
We pretended like we made up lyrics on the spot,
but we just recited obscure Public Enemy lines and they were astounded.

Soon we are sneaking spy photos of men in speedos in the English Garden
in Munich. Some men do not appreciate it. Some do. We ran.

Soon we are trying to kiss gorgeous Swedish girls
but one is named Lisa and one is named Liza.
They both vanish into the fog and potion of morning.

Soon we are in Vienna, inventing Irish Shanties
and the bar mumbles along enthusiastically.
"Oh the pants they do be dropping
and the fish are always gay
and I'll show no signs of stopping
what's up with these toilets- you're gay!"

We are grown men.

Soon we are dancing on a train to Holland and no one can hear the music.

Poetry never happens in a book.

THIS IS HOW IT FELT

1918

When we were stamps and paper,
she tattooed a year on her arm: 1918,
the year time zones were made law by train companies for America.
She imagined us above time.

I felt the thing roar along the tunnels of my ears,
like Santa Ana winds through a pipe organ.

She hissed a heavy weather kiss into me
like a child whispering into a stethoscope:

I need you.

We would drive as far as we could afford,
her eyes illuminating the yellow french fries
streaming under our car
along the dark interstate.

We tried to call it something.
What tried to name this feeling between being born alone and being dead.
We drove through every cemetery
until we realized
there are still birds flying the world
without names.

I fell into a swimming pool of water and engraved bullets.
Holding my breath, I imagined all those knuckle-dragging stiletto monkeys
who tried to take you out and tried to take you from me.
I found our names on some 50 cal. rounds and swam to the surface.

Your parents' stubborn will,
your parents' bloodlines and quiet disappointment
could not steal it.

I know your father loved the car more than you.
Still, he couldn't keep it running.

We drive to make the car something good again.
Bullets hanging from the rear view mirror.
We are brief.

MY SPEECH TO THE GRADUATING CLASS

For the advancing ones.

I might have written it somewhere else
maybe in another poem
but it might be a nice way to start off this
shindig.

You belong everywhere.

The age you are at right now is something you will want back in about ten
years.
Try and be less reserved.
Be bold now. Tell her you've got a crush, or had a crush and if they make the
right face then you still have that crush. It's OK. She won't stab your face.

This is a neat time, the age of exploration.
I was a desperate explorer.
I ain't talking about Robitussin overdoses and turning an apple into a bong.
I am talking exploring limits and setting your boundaries. I am talking about
toilet papering someone's house you love. Ding dong ditching the mayor.
Take a lawn gnome hostage but not chopping it into dust, boundaries.
The parents will forgive you. The cops will forget you. You are young and that
has value. And the value is $29.95.

Get a journal. You should document this era cause the upcoming changes are
shocking. Punks will become political activists in suits, Hippies will become
business people for environmental agencies, Skaters will become graphic
designers, Football stars will become glow in the dark pastors, Band kids will
become ninjas, Cheerleaders will become employees for Cold Stone Cream-
ery. Maybe journal it all cause you will forget. The future will seem so differ-
ent. Teens in the future are going to listen to carnival music and you'll say,
"...aw back in my day."

No matter how cool you were at your coolest peak of high school, in 4 years
you will look back at photos and say, "Lordy I was a big dork." You're not a
dork. But you'll think that. Its OK .This will give you the rush of humility.
This is good. Be proud of how humble you can be.

Some of you are off to college. Screw you.

College is not a passport to success. A passport is not a passport to success. Delaying self-gratification is.

Learn how to not want it now.

Studies show that the main thing that plagues our generation is that we don't know how to delay self- gratification. If we can learn to save money, organize a game plan, read, clean up our lives, floss once in awhile, then we will rule the world.

You will forget your locker combos, the concept of popularity and the vale-dictorians speech. You will remember the teachers who cared for you and you will remember being able to eat Taco Bell like an aardvark without barfing up any ants.

You want to be a doctor. You' might end up working at Chili's. At least for awhile. So what? Try the steak fajita pita. You're working and there is honor in labor.

There are jobs out there you don't have to hate. You will hate your first few jobs. Pretend it's a game. Pretend you love hardship. "You want me to stay an extra hour? How about two hours!" Make sure you collect your overtime. Write stuff down.

Let's not be scared about the future. Let's be scared about our bodies getting even wonkier and weirder.

The Military is not what they are telling you. It can change you for the better. It can change you for the worse. It will definitely let you shower with many naked people. At once.

The end of high school is not freedom. A soaring, screaming, bald eagle with a cape is freedom and freedom needs food.

It is as hard to forget the bad stuff as it is to remember the good stuff. You will forget a lot about this time. Remember the hallway make outs. Forget the wedgies. Most bully's end up on court TV anyway.

Forget all that crap about the journey not the destination.
Learn how to meet good people, try and remember their names
and treat them well. Die happy if you die surrounded.
You will forget peoples names. Only jerks don't understand this.

Really cool people don't know they are cool.

Some people will try to kick your face in. Know when to kick back and know when to tell your friends you punched someone's foot with your face.

Even drug dealers think users are annoying.

Don't think about sex more than you have to. Your parents think you don't ever touch anybody.

As far as writing a virginity pact. You don't need some pact to stay a virgin if that's your thing. Over 14,000 get busy after the first year of making a virginity pact. A pact or vow does nothing if you are lying to yourself. Also, SEX CAN SCREW YOU UP IF YOU HAVE TOO MUCH TOO EARLY WITH THE WRONG PEOPLE.

A Grad speaker once said wear sunscreen. I would like to add to please don't use the sunscreen that stays white on your nose. It looks like you cried glue.

Learn something every year or your mind will die at a television altar.

If your friend gets cancer treatment, shave your head.

Young love has about a 20% chance of success. Unless you're in the South where it is mandatory to get married at 19. Try to not get so broken up about it.

18-21 is a massive change. So is 21-25. Fall in a true love around 25. Date and learn about what you need before that. Kiss with all your might.

Tell strangers nice things about their eyes or clothes. You will change their day.

Some people are drawn to drama. You are not community theater. Fire the actors from your life. Just cause you know someone doesn't mean you owe them anything. Especially if they're a tool.

Ladies. Tell men exactly what you want. They are simple creatures. They do not read into things. Take him to dinner.
Gentlemen. Tell her how you feel a lot. Notice details about her and say you noticed it. Ask questions and just listen and hold. Plan things. You still might get it wrong.

Some ladies are weird until about 24, 25. Chicks on the wrong birth control or Xanax are even weirder. Trust me on this.

If you don't know what you want to be, so what. You will fall into something. Just do something or you're just a gassy little speed bump. You want to be an artist or photographer, or writer? Don't worry about being good, just begin.

Realize that guilt has guided very smart people in the wrong direction.

Imagine what it is like raising kids. Know that it's hard. Let your parents know you know this. They may cry. Being alive is expensive and they wanted you more than those fancy romantic vacations. This should make you feel good.

Always have poor friends or acquaintances. It makes the purchasing of luxury automobiles and useless gadgetry ridiculous when people are desperate.

Somewhere, someone is desperate.

Some people aren't very good at laughing. They will be mad at you. Wonder how they got that way and keep laughing. Maybe not in their face. No one loves a spittle spaz.

Ask old people how they're doing. The answer will be long. This will help you slow down.

Go to other countries. Not a typical backpacking tour. Planned tour means you will hang with Americans on bikes and flirt with drunk Germans and someone will steal your Levi's in the hostel and a guy from Poland will sock you in the face while bad techno plays everywhere and you will learn nothing except that your face hurts and not everyone showers. Get into other cultures and talk politics and love.

Meeting other people is the only way to know if you believe what you believe cause it's been handed to you, or if it really rings true in your heart.

Getting lost should be seen as a sweet chance to be found.

Remember, you belong everywhere.

Derrick Brown was a paratrooper for the 82nd Airborne Artillery. He is ordained to perform weddings. He has been published in 4 countries and has won various international writing awards for his poetry. He was a gondolier in Long Beach, CA, a weatherman in Flagstaff, a magician in California and now lives outside of Nashville Tennessee. You may see Derrick touring the U.S on his motorcycle to get to the next reading. He loves your face.

9 780978 998912